Flip-Flop Accents

Design

Size: **Diamond Bows:** 3 inches W x ½ inch H x 1½ inches D (7.6cm x 1.3cm x 3.8cm), including acrylic stones
Intertwining Angles: 2¾ inches W x ½ inch H x 2¾ inches D (7cm x 1.3cm x 7cm), including pompom
Sunbursts: 3½ inches W x ½ inch H x 3½ inches D (8.9cm x 1.3cm x 8.9cm), including acrylic stone
Two-Toned Bows: 3⅞ inches W x ⅜ inch H x 2⅜ inches D (9.8cm x 1cm x 6cm), including acrylic stones
Skill Level: Beginner

Materials

Each
❑ Plastic canvas yarn as listed in color key
❑ Pair of flip-flops to coordinate with accent colors
❑ Hot-glue gun

Diamond Bows
❑ Small amounts 7-count plastic canvas: bright pink and bright purple
❑ Small amount bright pink plastic canvas yarn
❑ 4 (15 x 7 mm) crystal foil-backed navette acrylic faceted stones

Intertwining Angles
❑ Small amounts 7-count plastic canvas: blue, green, red and yellow
❑ Small amount blue, green, red or yellow plastic canvas yarn
❑ 2 (½-inch/13mm) red tinsel pompoms

Sunbursts
❑ Small amounts 7-count plastic canvas: bright orange and yellow
❑ Small amount orange plastic canvas yarn
❑ 2 (18 x 13 mm) topaz foil-backed oval acrylic faceted stones

Two-Toned Bows
❑ Small amounts 7-count plastic canvas: black and red
❑ Small amount black or red plastic canvas yarn
❑ 2 (18 x 13 mm) ruby foil-backed oval acrylic faceted stones
❑ 4 (7 mm) ruby foil-backed round acrylic faceted stones
❑ Red and white thread

Stitching Step by Step
Diamond Bows

1 Cut top (first), third and bottom (fifth) bows from bright purple plastic canvas; cut second and fourth bows from bright pink plastic canvas according to graphs (page 3). Pieces will remain unstitched.

2 For each of the two bows, place one each of the five bow pieces together from top to bottom, aligning centers of bows (at arrows). Using bright pink yarn and leaving a tail at beginning of stitch, stitch through all five pieces where indicated on top bow graph, then wrap yarn around pieces at center two times, leaving a tail. Thread ending tail under wraps on back side, then tie tails together in a knot.

3 Glue two crystal navette stones to each top bow where indicated on graph with blue lines.

4 Glue diamond bows to center tops of straps on coordinating flip-flops.

Intertwining Angles

1 Cut one angle each for each flip-flop from blue, green, red and yellow plastic canvas according to graph (page 4). Pieces will remain unstitched.

2 Following Fig. 1 (page 4), place blue angle on top of yellow angle. Bring arms of yellow angle up over arms of blue angle. Following Fig. 2 (page 4), place red angle on top of green angle. Bring arms of green angle up over arms of red angle.

3 Following Fig. 3 (page 4), place red and green angles under blue and yellow angles. Using red yarn, stitch through all four angles where indicated on angle graph, securing yarn on back side.

4 Repeat steps 2 and 3 for second accent.

5 Glue red pompom to top of each blue angle where indicated on graph.

6 Glue intertwining angles to center tops of straps on coordinating flip-flops.

Sunbursts

1 Cut four large rays each from yellow and orange plastic canvas and four small rays each from yellow and orange plastic canvas according to graphs (page 4). Pieces will remain unstitched.

2 Place small yellow rays together, forming an X; place small orange rays together, forming an X. Following Fig. 4 (page 4) place small orange rays behind small yellow rays. Repeat with large rays.

3 Following Fig. 5 (page 4), place large rays behind small rays. Using orange yarn and leaving tails at beginning and end of stitches, stitch as needed through all four pieces in center of sunburst to secure. Tie tails together in a knot.

4 Following Fig. 6 (page 4), glue one topaz oval stone to top of each sunburst where indicated with green lines.

5 Glue sunbursts to center tops of straps on coordinating flip-flops.

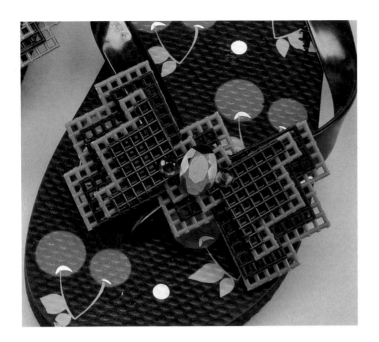

Two-Toned Bows

1 Cut top (first) and third bows from black plastic canvas; cut second and bottom (fourth) bows from red plastic canvas according to graphs (page 5). Pieces will remain unstitched.

2 For each bow, place a third bow on a bottom bow where indicated with blue lines. Place a second bow on the third bow where indicated with green lines. Place a top bow on the second bow where indicated with blue lines. Using black yarn and leaving a tail at beginning and end of stitch, stitch through all four pieces where indicated on top bow graph. Tie tails together in a knot.

3 Glue one ruby oval stone and two ruby round stones to each top bow where indicated on graph with red lines.

4 Glue two-toned bows to center tops of straps on coordinating flip-flops.

Diamond Top (First) Bow
6 holes x 6 holes
Cut 2 from bright purple
Do not stitch

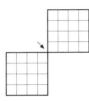

Diamond Second Bow
8 holes x 8 holes
Cut 2 from bright pink
Do not stitch

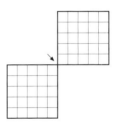

Diamond Third Bow
10 holes x 10 holes
Cut 2 from bright purple
Do not stitch

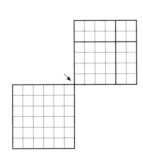

Diamond Fourth Bow
12 holes x 12 holes
Cut 2 from bright pink
Do not stitch

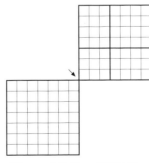

Diamond Bottom (Fifth) Bow
14 holes x 14 holes
Cut 2 from bright purple
Do not stitch

COLOR KEY	
Yards	**Plastic Canvas Yarn**
1 (1m)	▒ Bright pink
1 (1m)	■ Red
1 (1m)	▒ Orange
1 (1m)	■ Black
	⁄ Attach crystal navette stone
	● Attach red pompom
	○ Attach topaz oval stone
	○ Attach ruby oval stone
	○ Attach ruby round stone

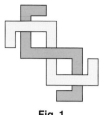

Fig. 1

Fig. 2

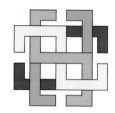

Fig. 3

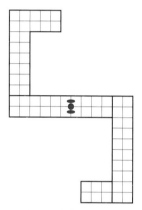

Intertwining Angle
12 holes x 18 holes
Cut 2 each from blue,
green, red and yellow
Do not stitch

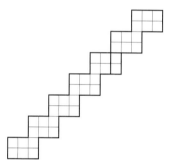

Sunburst Large Ray
15 holes x 14 holes
Cut 4 each from
yellow and orange
Do not stitch

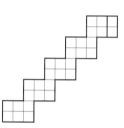

Sunburst Small Ray
11 holes x 10 holes
Cut 4 each from
yellow and orange
Do not stitch

Fig. 4

Fig. 5

Fig. 6

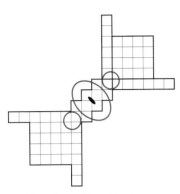

Two-Toned Top (First) Bow
16 holes x 16 holes
Cut 2 from black
Do not stitch

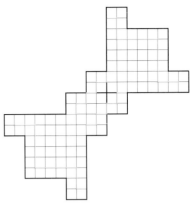

Two-Toned Second Bow
18 holes x 18 holes
Cut 2 from red
Do not stitch

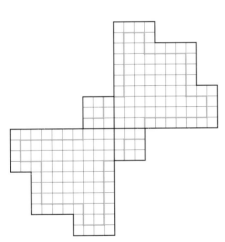

Two-Toned Third Bow
20 holes x 20 holes
Cut 2 from black
Do not stitch

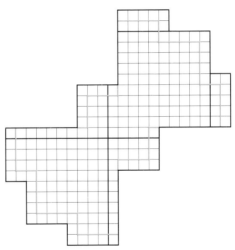

Two-Toned Bottom (Fourth) Bow
22 holes x 22 holes
Cut 2 from red
Do not stitch

COLOR KEY

Yards	Plastic Canvas Yarn
1 (1m)	▨ Bright pink
1 (1m)	■ Red
1 (1m)	▨ Orange
1 (1m)	■ Black
	⬭ Attach crystal navette stone
	● Attach red pompom
	○ Attach topaz oval stone
	○ Attach ruby oval stone
	○ Attach ruby round stone

Picnic Trio

Designs by Rosemarie Walter

Size:
Cup Stacker: 10¾ inches H x 4¼ inches in diameter (27.3cm x 10.8cm)

Napkin Holder: 7¼ inches W x 5¼ inches H x 2⅝ inches D (18.4cm x 13.3cm x 6.7cm)

Utensil Caddy: 6¼ inches W x 7¾ inches H x 6¼ inches D (15.9cm x 19.7cm x 15.9cm), including handle

Skill Level:
Intermediate

Materials

❑ 4 sheets white 7-count plastic canvas
❑ 4 (4½-inch) Darice plastic canvas radial circles
❑ 3 (3-inch) Darice plastic canvas radial circles
❑ Uniek Needloft plastic canvas as listed in color key

Stitching Step by Step

1 Cut one cup stacker, one each of napkin holder front and back, two napkin holder ends, one utensil caddy handle and three utensil caddies from plastic canvas according to graphs (pages 8–10). Cut one 47-hole x 17-hole piece for napkin holder base. Base will remain unstitched.

2 Cut three cup stacker braces from 4½-inch radial circles following graph (page 9), cutting away gray areas. Cut the outermost row of holes from remaining 4½-inch radial circle for cup stacker base (no graph). Do not cut 3-inch radial circles (utensil caddy bases). Bases and stacker braces will remain unstitched.

3 Stitch napkin holder pieces following graphs. Using white, Whipstitch front and back to ends, then Whipstitch front, back and ends to unstitched base; Overcast top edges.

4 Roll cup stacker in a cylinder, overlapping one hole along side edges; stitch together as shown with white stitches.

5 Stitch flowers on utensil caddy pieces, stitching one as graphed and one each replacing pink with sail blue and lilac. Roll each caddy in a cylinder, overlapping seven holes; stitch together with white stitches as shown. Work forest Running Stitches where indicated.

Cup Stacker Assembly

1 Following Fig. 1 and graph throughout assembly, and using white through step 2, Whipstitch unstitched base to bottom edge of cup stacker.

2 Whipstitch braces in place where indicated on graph with red lines and to top edge.

3 Work flowers and Running Stitches following graph. Overcast edges of front opening with white.

Utensil Caddy Assembly

1 Following Fig. 2 and graphs throughout assembly, Whipstitch one utensil caddy base to bottom of each caddy as in step A.

2 Place caddies 1–3 together with seams facing center and flowers facing out.

3 Using white through step 7 and following step B, Whipstitch caddies 1 and 2 together. Continue following red arrows around caddy 2 to caddy 3, Overcasting top edge.

4 Whipstitch caddies 2 and 3 together. Continue following red arrows around caddy 3 to caddy 1, Overcasting top edge.

5 Whipstitch caddies 3 and 1 together. Continue following red arrows around caddy 1 to beginning stitches, Overcasting top edge.

6 Overcast top edges of caddies in center area inside green box.

7 If desired, tack caddies together with white a few holes beneath forest Running Stitches.

8 Work forest Running Stitches on handle. Fold handle in half with wrong sides together. Insert ends of handle inside center area; tack in place with white.

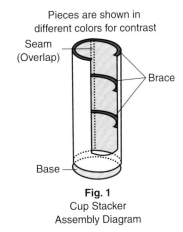

Pieces are shown in
different colors for contrast

Seam
(Overlap)

Brace

Base

Fig. 1
Cup Stacker
Assembly Diagram

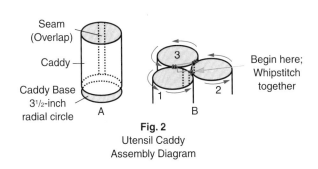

Seam
(Overlap)

Caddy

Caddy Base
3½-inch
radial circle

A

B

Begin here;
Whipstitch
together

Fig. 2
Utensil Caddy
Assembly Diagram

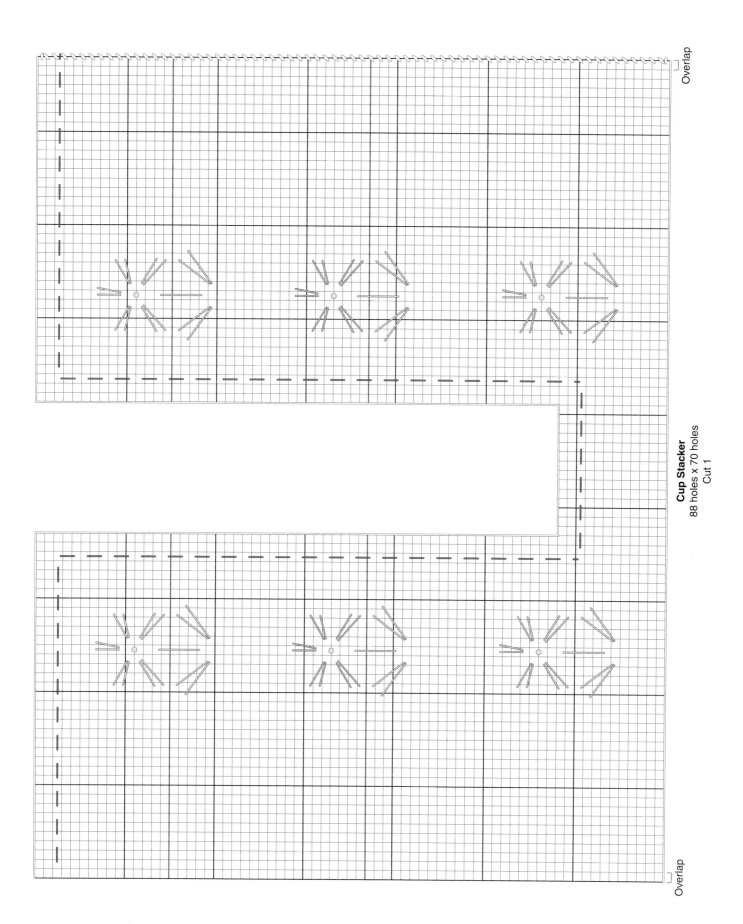

Cup Stacker
88 holes x 70 holes
Cut 1

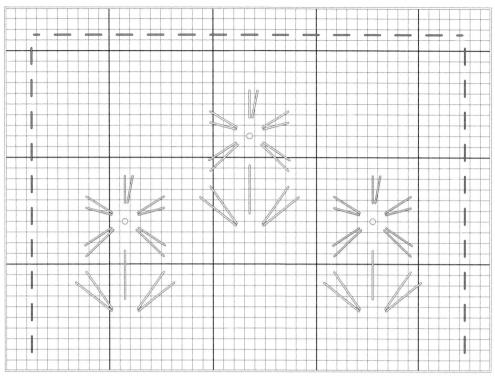

Napkin Holder Front & Back
47 holes x 34 holes
Cut 2

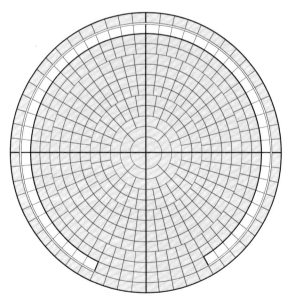

Cup Stacker Brace
Cut 3 from 4¹/₂-inch radial circles,
cutting away gray area
Do not stitch

COLOR KEY

Yards	Plastic Canvas Yarn
30 (27.5)	☐ White #41
3 (2.8)	⁄ Pink #07 Straight Stitch
8 (7.4m)	⁄ Fern #23 Straight Stitch
10 (9.2m)	⁄ Forest #29 Running Stitch
3 (2.8)	⁄ Sail blue #35 Straight Stitch
3 (2.8)	⁄ Lilac #45 Straight Stitch
4 (3.7m)	○ Yellow #57 (2-wrap) French Knot

Color numbers given are for Uniek Needloft plastic canvas yarn.

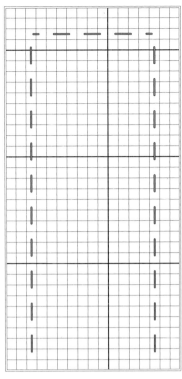

Napkin Holder End
17 holes x 34 holes
Cut 2

COLOR KEY

Yards	Plastic Canvas Yarn
30 (27.5)	☐ White #41
3 (2.8)	╱ Pink #07 Straight Stitch
8 (7.4m)	╱ Fern #23 Straight Stitch
10 (9.2m)	╱ Forest #29 Running Stitch
3 (2.8)	╱ Sail blue #35 Straight Stitch
3 (2.8)	╱ Lilac #45 Straight Stitch
4 (3.7m)	○ Yellow #57 (2-wrap) French Knot

Color numbers given are for Uniek Needloft plastic canvas yarn.

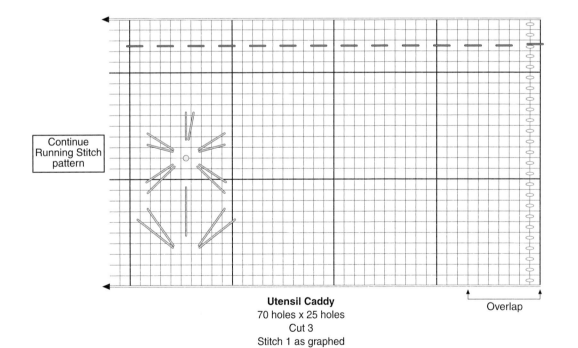

Continue Running Stitch pattern

Utensil Caddy
70 holes x 25 holes
Cut 3
Stitch 1 as graphed
Stitch 1 each replacing pink with sail blue and lilac

Overlap

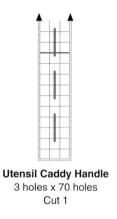

Utensil Caddy Handle
3 holes x 70 holes
Cut 1

Butterfly Windsock

Design by Andy Ashley

Size: 7⅛ inches W x 37 inches H x 4¼ inches D
(18.1cm x 88.8cm x 10.8cm), including
ribbon and hanger

Skill Level: Intermediate

Materials

❑ 1 sheet each purple and pastel green
7-count plastic canvas
❑ Small amount lavender and black
7-count plastic canvas
❑ Uniek Needloft plastic canvas yarn as listed
in color key
❑ 4½ yards (4.1m) 1½-inch-wide (39mm) ribbon
in coordinating colors
❑ 1-inch (2.5cm) gold ring
❑ 6 inches (15.2cm) black chenille stem
❑ Monofilament
❑ Craft glue

Stitching Step by Step

1 Cut one cylinder from pastel green plastic canvas, one butterfly and two bands from purple plastic canvas, two wings from lavender plastic canvas and one body from black plastic canvas according to graphs (pages 12 and 13).

2 Overlap three holes on side edges of cylinder and stitch together with fern Continental Stitches.

3 Use photo as a guide through step 8. Place one purple band around top of cylinder where indicated with red lines, having ends meet at seam. Stitch in place with bright purple Running Stitches as shown on band graph. Repeat with remaining purple band at bottom of cylinder.

4 Place wings on butterfly where indicated with pink lines. Stitch in place with bright purple Running Stitches as shown on wing graph.

5 Thread ends of chenille stem from back to front on head of butterfly. Pull through and curl ends.

6 Place black body on butterfly where indicated with blue lines. Center assembled butterfly on cylinder opposite seam. Stitch in place through all three layers with black Running Stitches, working stitches on top and bottom of body without attaching to cylinder.

7 Cut ribbon in eight 20¼-inch (51.4cm) lengths. Evenly space and glue about ¼ inch (0.6cm) of each length inside cylinder around bottom edge.

8 Cut four 14-inch (35.6cm) lengths of monofilament. Evenly space four lengths around top edge of cylinder; thread through holes and tie in a knot. Tie remaining ends in a knot around 1-inch (2.5cm) gold ring, keeping lengths even.

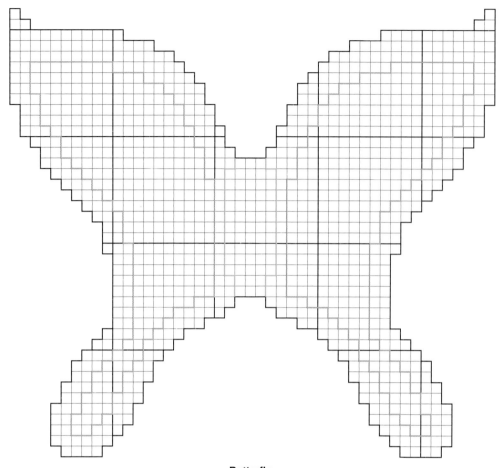

Butterfly
47 holes x 42 holes
Cut 1 from purple
Do not stitch

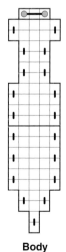

Body
5 holes x 21 holes
Cut 1 from black

COLOR KEY

Yards	Plastic Canvas Yarn
1 (1m)	☐ Fern #23
1 (1m)	✎ Black #00 Running Stitch
5 (4.6m)	✎ Bright purple #64 Running Stitch
	◉ Attach chenille stem

Color numbers given are for Uniek Needloft plastic canvas yarn.

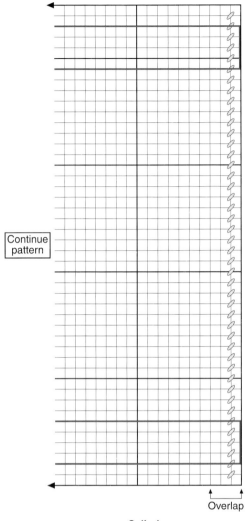

Cylinder
90 holes x 45 holes
Cut 1 from pastel green

Continue pattern

Overlap

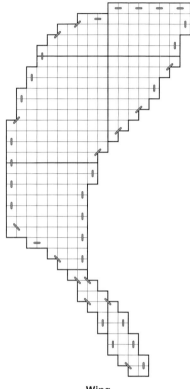

Wing
18 holes x 35 holes
Cut 2 from lavender

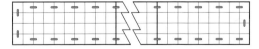

Band
89 holes x 4 holes
Cut 2 from purple

Animal Baskets

Designs by Sandra Miller Maxfield

Size: **Chicken Basket:** 5¾ inches W x 9⅛ inches H x 6¾ inches D (14.6cm x 23.2cm x 17.1cm)
Cat Basket: 5¾ inches W x 9 inches H x 6½ inches D (14.6cm x 22.9cm x 16.5cm)
Dog Basket: 7⅝ inches W x 9½ inches H x 6 inches D (19.4cm x 24.1cm x 15.2cm)
Inner Baskets: 5⅜ inches H x 3 inches in diameter (13.7cm x 7.6cm)

Skill Level: Intermediate

Materials

- ❏ 2 sheets clear 7-count plastic canvas
- ❏ 1½ sheet black 7-count plastic canvas
- ❏ 1 sheet each brown and bright yellow 7-count plastic canvas
- ❏ ½ sheet dark blue 7-count plastic canvas
- ❏ ¼ sheet red and tan 7-count plastic canvas
- ❏ Small amounts orange and pastel green 7-count plastic canvas
- ❏ 3 (4½-inch/11.4cm) plastic canvas radial circles
- ❏ Uniek Needloft plastic canvas as listed in color key

Stitching Step by Step

Chicken

1 Cut one right eye and one left eye from clear plastic canvas, one hat brim and one bow tie from dark blue plastic canvas, and one beak top and one beak bottom from orange plastic canvas according to graphs (page 17). Cut one outer basket from bright yellow plastic canvas according to graph (page 20), cutting out the 12 holes shown in white. Hat brim and beak pieces will remain unstitched.

2 Also cut the following (no graphs): one 61-hole x 35-hole piece for inner basket from clear plastic canvas, one 4-hole x 70-hole piece for handle from bright yellow plastic canvas, and one 68-hole x 6-hole piece for hat side from dark blue plastic canvas. Cut the four outermost rows of holes from 4½-inch (11.4cm) circle for base. Inner basket, handle, hat side and base will remain unstitched.

3 Stitch and Overcast eyes and bow tie following graphs. Overlap 5 holes along short edges of outer basket as indicated; work yellow Backstitches through both layers where shown on graph to secure.

Cat Basket

1 Cut one muzzle from clear plastic canvas, two eyes from pastel green plastic canvas, and two ears from black plastic canvas according to graphs (page 18). Cut one outer basket from black plastic canvas according to graph (page 20), cutting out the 12 holes shown in white. Ears will remain unstitched.

2 Also cut the following (no graphs): one 61-hole x 35-hole piece for inner basket from clear plastic canvas, one 4-hole x 70-hole piece for handle from black plastic canvas, and one 68-hole x 3-hole piece for collar from red plastic canvas. Cut the four outermost rows of holes from 4½-inch (11.4cm) circle for base. Inner basket, handle, collar and base will remain unstitched.

3 Stitch and Overcast eyes and muzzle following graphs, but do not work center stitch on eyes at this time. Using black, Whipstitch dart on one ear together; Overcast remaining edges. Reverse second ear before Whipstitching dart together; Overcast remaining edges.

4 Using black through step 5, overlap 5 holes along short edges of outer basket as indicated; work Backstitches through both layers where shown on graph to secure.

4 Use photo as a guide throughout assembly. Using bright orange and easing to fit, Whipstitch top and bottom beaks to front strip where indicated with green loop, folding beaks where indicated on graphs. *Note: Small orange line, dividing the loop, is where top and bottom beaks meet.* Center eyes between strips on outer basket; tack in place with black.

5 Whipstitch 35-hole edges of inner basket together with white. Slip inner basket into outer basket, placing seams together. *Note: Seam side is the back side.*

6 Using yellow throughout, Whipstitch bottom edges of inner and outer baskets to unstitched base, working through all three layers; Whipstitch top edges of baskets together.

7 Using dark royal throughout, tack bow tie through both basket layers where indicated on graph. Whipstitch short ends of hat side together. Whipstitch bottom edge of hat side to inner edge of hat brim. Overcast remaining edges of assembled hat.

8 Place handle ends inside inner basket; Backstitch in place through all three layers with yellow.

9 Slide hat down over handle and top of basket.

5 Use photo as a guide throughout assembly. Tack bottom edges of ears to outer basket where indicated with red lines. Place top edge of muzzle on front strip where indicated on graph; tack in place. Place eyes on outer basket where indicated with pink lines; attach to strips by working the center stitch.

6 Whipstitch 35-hole edges of inner basket together with white. Slip inner basket into outer basket, placing seams together. *Note: Seam side is the back side.*

7 Using black throughout, Whipstitch bottom edges of inner and outer baskets to unstitched base, working through all three layers; Whipstitch top edges of baskets together.

8 Place handle ends outside basket; Backstitch in place through all three layers with black.

9 Whipstitch short ends of collar together with Christmas red. Slip collar up over bottom of basket.

Dog Basket

1 Cut one muzzle, one dog tag and two eyes from clear plastic canvas; two ears from black plastic canvas; and one tongue from red plastic canvas according to graphs (pages 19). Cut one outer basket from brown plastic canvas according to graph (page 20), cutting out the 12 holes shown in white. Ears will remain unstitched.

2 Also cut the following (no graphs): one 61-hole x 35-hole piece for inner basket from clear plastic canvas, one 4-hole x 70-hole piece for handle from brown plastic canvas, and one 68-hole x 3-hole piece for collar from tan plastic canvas. Cut the four outermost rows of holes from 4½-inch (11.4cm) circle for base. Inner basket, handle, collar and base will remain unstitched.

3 Stitch and Overcast eyes, muzzle, tongue and dog tag following graphs. Using black, Overcast around side and bottom edges of ears with black.

4 Using brown throughout, overlap 5 holes along short edges of outer basket as indicated; work Backstitches through both layers where shown on graph to secure.

5 Use photo as a guide throughout assembly. Using black, tack tongue behind muzzle as shown in Fig. 1 (page 19). Position top edge of muzzle where indicated on graph; tack muzzle (and tongue, if desired) in place with black. Position top edge of eyes where indicated with purple lines; tack eyes in place.

6 Whipstitch 35-hole edges of inner basket together with white. Slip inner basket into outer basket, placing seams together. *Note: Seam side is the back side.*

7 Using brown throughout, Whipstitch bottom edges of inner and outer baskets to unstitched base, working through all three layers; Whipstitch top edges of baskets together, attaching top edge of ears in place where indicated while Whipstitching.

8 Place handle ends inside inner basket; Backstitch in place through all three layers with brown.

9 Whipstitch short ends of collar together with brown. Seam is back of collar. Using black, tack top edge of dog tag where indicated to front bottom edge of collar. Slip collar up over bottom of basket.

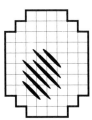

Chicken Left Eye
8 holes x 10 holes
Cut 1 from clear

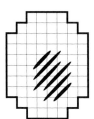

Chicken Right Eye
8 holes x 10 holes
Cut 1 from clear

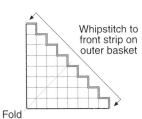

Whipstitch to
front strip on
outer basket

Fold

Chicken Beak Bottom
8 holes x 8 holes
Cut 1 from orange
Do not stitch

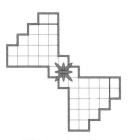

Chicken Bow Tie
11 holes x 11 holes
Cut 1 from dark blue

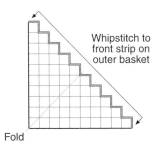

Whipstitch to
front strip on
outer basket

Fold

Chicken Beak Top
10 holes x 10 holes
Cut 1 from orange
Do not stitch

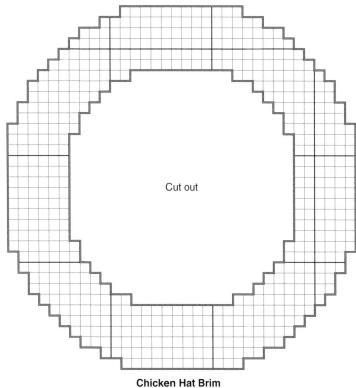

Cut out

Chicken Hat Brim
34 holes x 34 holes
Cut 1 from dark blue
Do not stitch

COLOR KEY

Yards	Plastic Canvas Yarn
18 (16.5m)	■ Black #00
1 (1m)	■ Christmas red #02
8 (7.4m)	■ Dark royal #48
2 (1.9m)	⁄ Brown #15 Overcast and Whipstitch
4 (3.7m)	⁄ White #41 Whipstitch
2 (1.9m)	⁄ Yellow #57 Backstitch, Overcast and Whipstitch
1 (1m)	⁄ Bright orange #58 Whipstitch
	● Attach bow tie
	● Attach cat muzzle
	○ Attach dog muzzle

Color numbers given are for Uniek Needloft
plastic canvas yarn.

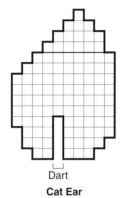

Cat Ear
10 holes x 14 holes
Cut 2, reverse 1, from black
Do not stitch

Dart

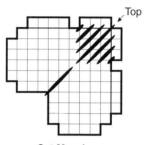

Top

Cat Muzzle
11 holes x 11 holes
Cut 1 from clear

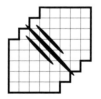

Cat Eye
8 holes x 8 holes
Cut 2 from pastel green

COLOR KEY	
Yards	**Plastic Canvas Yarn**
18 (16.5m)	■ Black #00
1 (1m)	■ Christmas red #02
8 (7.4m)	■ Dark royal #48
2 (1.9m)	▱ Brown #15 Overcast and Whipstitch
4 (3.7m)	▱ White #41 Whipstitch
2 (1.9m)	▱ Yellow #57 Backstitch, Overcast and Whipstitch
1 (1m)	▱ Bright orange #58 Whipstitch
	● Attach bow tie
	● Attach cat muzzle
	○ Attach dog muzzle

Color numbers given are for Uniek Needloft plastic canvas yarn.

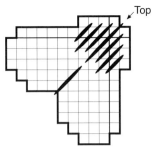

Dog Muzzle
12 holes x 12 holes
Cut 1 from clear

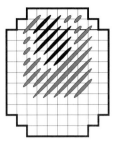

Dog Eye
10 holes x 12 holes
Cut 2 from clear

Dog Tongue
6 holes x 7 holes
Cut 1 from red

Attach to
dog collar

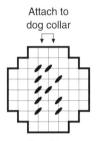

Dog Tag
8 holes x 8 holes
Cut 1 from clear

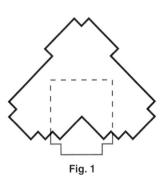

Fig. 1

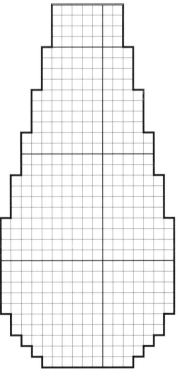

Dog Ear
17 holes x 34 holes
Cut 2 from black
Do not stitch

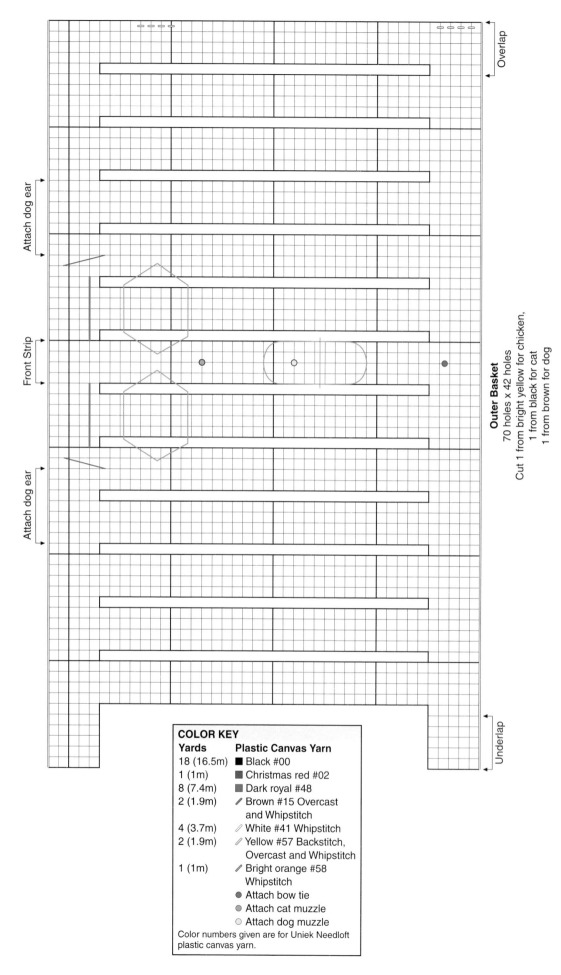

Overlap

Attach dog ear

Front Strip

Attach dog ear

Underlap

Outer Basket
70 holes x 42 holes
Cut 1 from bright yellow for chicken,
1 from black for cat
1 from brown for dog

COLOR KEY

Yards	Plastic Canvas Yarn
18 (16.5m)	■ Black #00
1 (1m)	■ Christmas red #02
8 (7.4m)	■ Dark royal #48
2 (1.9m)	⁄ Brown #15 Overcast and Whipstitch
4 (3.7m)	⁄ White #41 Whipstitch
2 (1.9m)	⁄ Yellow #57 Backstitch, Overcast and Whipstitch
1 (1m)	⁄ Bright orange #58 Whipstitch
	● Attach bow tie
	● Attach cat muzzle
	○ Attach dog muzzle

Color numbers given are for Uniek Needloft plastic canvas yarn.

White Lace Set

Designs by Fran Rohus

Size:

Basket: 9½ inches W x 8¾ inches H x
4⅝ inches D (24.1cm x 22.2cm x 11.7cm),
including handle
Coasters: 4¾ inches square (12.1cm)
Coaster Holder: 5⅛ inches W x 3 inches H x
1⅝ inches D (13cm x 7.6cm x 4.1cm)

Skill Level: Intermediate

Materials

❑ 3 sheets white 7-count plastic canvas
❑ Plastic canvas yarn as listed in color key
❑ 9 x 12-inch (22.9 x 30.5cm) sheet pink felt
❑ Craft glue or hot-glue gun

Stitching Step by Step

1 Cut plastic canvas according to graphs (pages 22–24), cutting out gray areas, giving particular care to the "lace" edges.

2 Cut one 53-hole x 23-hole piece for basket base, one 33-hole x 14-hole piece for coaster holder front and one 33-hole x 10-hole piece for coaster holder base (no graphs). All but basket ends will remain unstitched.

3 Cut three 3¾-inch (9.6cm) squares of pink felt.

4 Use white through step 6. For basket, Whipstitch front and back to ends; Whipstitch front, back and ends to base.

5 Overlap handle pieces where indicated with blue shading; Backstitch together. Place handle ends inside basket ends where indicated with red lines; Backstitch in place as shown on basket end graph.

6 Whipstitch holder front and back to sides; Whipstitch front, back and sides to holder base.

7 Center and glue felt to coasters.

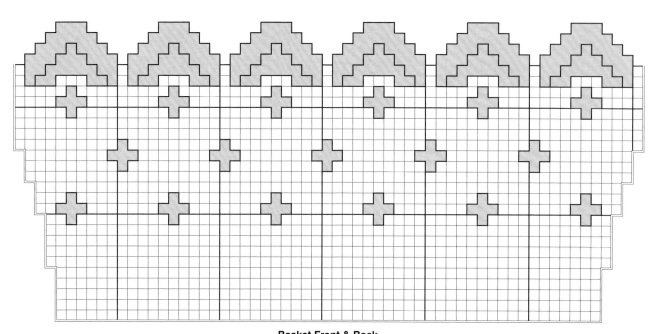

Basket Front & Back
61 holes x 28 holes
Cut 2,
cutting away gray areas
Do not stitch

COLOR KEY		
Yards	**Plastic Canvas Yarn**	
10 (9.2m)	✎	White Backstitch and Whipstitch

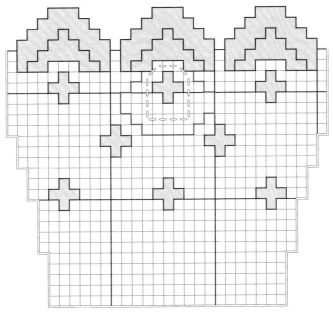

Basket End
31 holes x 28 holes
Cut 2,
cutting away gray areas

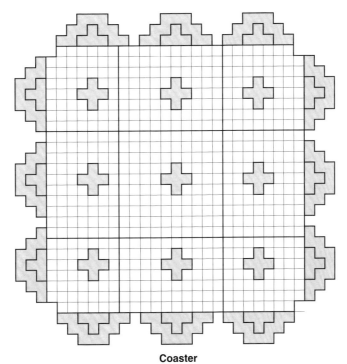

Coaster
31 holes x 31 holes
Cut 3,
cutting away gray areas

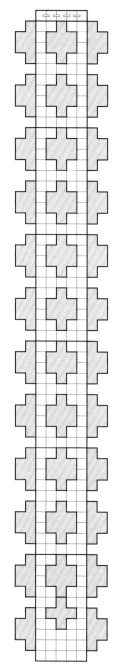

Basket Handle
9 holes x 61 holes
Cut 2,
Cutting away gray areas

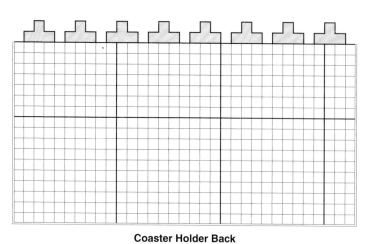

Coaster Holder Back
33 holes x 19 holes
Cut 1,
cutting away gray areas
Do not stitch

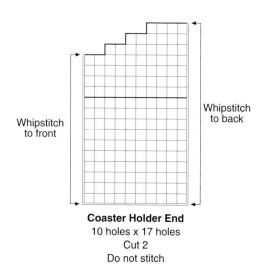

Whipstitch
to front

Whipstitch
to back

Coaster Holder End
10 holes x 17 holes
Cut 2
Do not stitch

COLOR KEY		
Yards	**Plastic Canvas Yarn**	
10 (9.2m)	⁄ White Backstitch and Whipstitch	

Key Rings

Designs by Andy Ashley

Size: **Car:** 5 inches W x 2⅞ inches H
(12.7cm x 7.3cm), including buttons
House: 4⅛ inches W x 3⅝ inches H
(10.5cm x 9.2cm)
Tennis Shoe: 3¾ inches W x 2¾ inches H
(9.5cm x 7cm)
Skill Level: Beginner

Materials

Each
❏ Uniek Needloft plastic canvas yarn as listed
in color key
❏ 1¼-inch silver split key ring
Car
❏ Small amounts 7-count plastic canvas:
bright yellow and purple
❏ 4 (1⅛-inch/28mm) bright pink buttons
House
❏ Small amounts 7-count plastic canvas:
dark blue, brown green and white
Tennis Shoe
❏ Small amounts 7-count plastic canvas:
red and white

Project Note

Stitch through all layers of plastic canvas. Weave yarn
tails under stitching on back sides of motifs or if needed,
tie yarn in small knots.

Stitching Step by Step

Car

1 Cut two cars from bright yellow plastic canvas;
cut two of each window from purple plastic canvas
according to graphs (page 26), cutting out small hole for
key ring on trunk of cars.

2 Hold car pieces together and work yellow Running
Stitches around car.

3 Place windows on both sides of car where indicated
with purple lines. *Note: On back side of car the
windows will be reversed.* Work bright purple Running
Stitches around windows as shown on graphs.

4 Attach buttons to both sides of car with bright pink
Straight Stitch where indicated, knotting yarn on
buttons on back side of car.

5 Attach key ring through hole in trunk of car.

House

1 Cut one house from dark blue plastic canvas according to graph, cutting out hole on right side of house below roof. Cut one roof from white plastic canvas, one door and one chimney from brown plastic canvas, and two bushes from green plastic canvas according to graphs. House will remain unstitched.

2 Place roof on house, aligning top edges; attach with black Backstitches as shown on roof graph. Place brown chimney on dark blue chimney and attach with brown backstitches as shown on chimney graph.

3 Place door on house where indicated with brown lines; attach with brown Backstitches as shown on door graph.

4 Place bushes on house where indicated with green lines. Attach with forest Backstitches as shown on bush graph. Work three Christmas red French Knots on each bush where desired.

5 Attach key ring through hole on right side of house.

Tennis Shoe

1 Cut two shoes from red plastic canvas; cut two soles and two patches from white plastic canvas according to graphs, cutting out small hole for key ring on upper left side of shoes.

2 Hold shoe pieces together and work Christmas red Running Stitches.

3 Place soles on both sides of shoe, matching bottom and front edges; attach with white Running Stitches as shown on sole graph.

4 Place patches on both sides of shoe where indicated with blue lines; attach with white Backstitches as shown on patch graph.

5 Cut an 18-inch (45.7cm) length of white yarn and lace through holes where indicated with white dots. Tie tails in a bow at top.

6 Attach key ring through hole on left side of shoe.

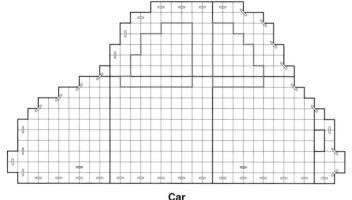

Car
33 holes x 17 holes
Cut 1 from bright yellow

Windshield
7 holes x 6 holes
Cut 2, reverse 1,
from purple

Back Window
5 holes x 6 holes
Cut 2, reverse 1,
from purple

COLOR KEY	
Yards	**Plastic Canvas Yarn**
2 (1.9m)	✦ Black #00 Backstitch
2 (1.9m)	✦ Christmas red #02 Running Stitch
2 (1.9m)	✦ Brown #15 Backstitch
1 (1m)	✦ Forest #29 Backstitch
2 (1.9m)	✦ White #41 Backstitch and Running Stitch
2 (1.9m)	✦ Yellow #57 Running Stitch
1 (1m)	✦ Bright pink #62 Straight Stitch
1 (1m)	✦ Bright purple #64 Running Stitch
	○ Attach white #41 shoe lace

Color numbers given are for Uniek Needloft plastic canvas yarn.

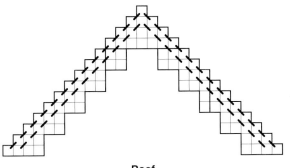

Roof
27 holes x 14 holes
Cut 1 from white

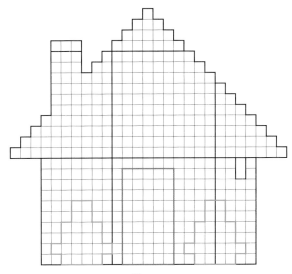

House
27 holes x 24 holes
Cut 1 from dark blue
Do not stitch

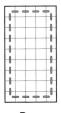

Door
5 holes x 9 holes
Cut 1 from brown

Bush
6 holes x 6 holes
Cut 2 from green

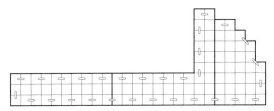

Sole
25 holes x 9 holes
Cut 2 from white

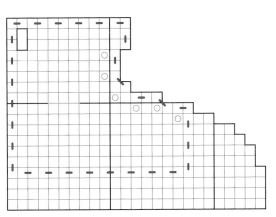

Tennis Shoe
25 holes x 18 holes
Cut 2 from red

Patch
5 holes x 5 holes
Cut 2 from white

Flower Basket

Design by Carol Nartowitz

Size: **Basket With Spokes:** Approximately 6⅝ inches H x 8¼ inches in diameter (16.8cm x 21cm)
Basket: 5⅝ inches H x 4¼ inches in diameter (14.3cm x 10.8cm)
Skill Level: Intermediate

Materials

❑ 2 sheets 7-count blue plastic canvas
❑ Uniek Needloft plastic canvas yarn as listed in color key
❑ ⅛-inch (3mm) satin ribbon as listed in color key
❑ ⅜-inch (9mm) satin ribbon as listed in color key
❑ Hot-glue gun

Stitching Step by Step

1 Cut plastic canvas according to graphs (pages 29 and 30), cutting out 36 small holes (in gray) at top of basket. Base and top spokes will remain unstitched.

2 Overlap two holes on side edges of basket and stitch together with Continental Stitches.

3 Leaving about 2 inches of ribbon on each end, weave ⅛-inch ribbon through each side spoke with a Running Stitch as shown; glue ends down on back sides of spokes.

4 Following Fig. 1 and using sail blue throughout assembly, Whipstitch top edges of side spokes to bars indicated on basket with red lines; Whipstitch bottom edges of spokes to bottom edge of basket where indicated with red lines, Whipstitching base in place at the same time.

5 Weave ⅜-inch (9mm) ribbon through holes on top of basket with a Running Stitch, going down at beginning hole, leaving a 9-inch tail and coming up at ending hole where indicated. Tie tails together in a bow; trim as desired.

6 Beginning on one side of seam, Whipstitch top spokes round top edge of basket; Overcast top edge between first and last spokes. Do not Overcast remaining edges on assembled basket.

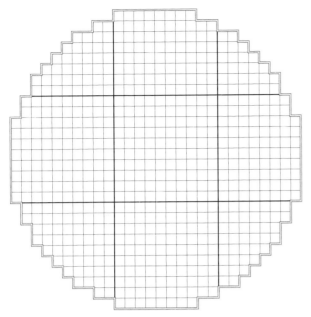

Base
28 holes x 28 holes
Cut 1
Do not stitch

COLOR KEY

Yards	Plastic Canvas Yarn
12 (11m)	☐ Sail blue #35
	¹/₈-Inch (3mm) Ribbon
6 (5.5m)	⧄ White
	³/₈-Inch (9mm) Ribbon
1 (1m)	⧄ White

Color number given is for Uniek
Needloft plastic canvas yarn.

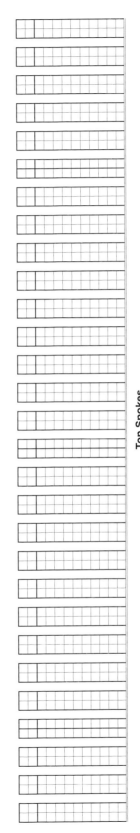

Top Spokes
86 holes x 12 holes
Cut 1
Do not stitch

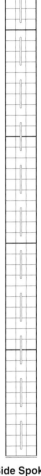

Side Spoke
3 holes x 44 holes
Cut 22

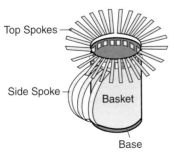

Top Spokes

Side Spoke

Basket

Base

Fig. 1

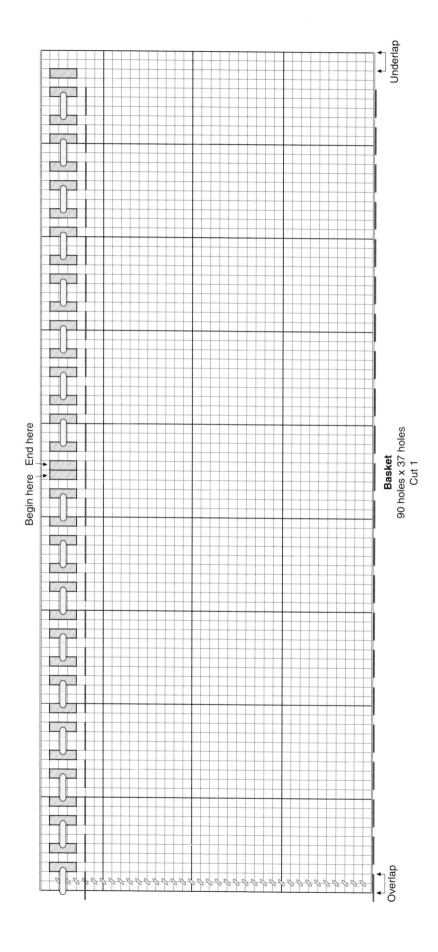

Basket
90 holes x 37 holes
Cut 1

Underlap

Begin here End here

Overlap

Cross Bookmarks

Designs by Sandra Maxfield

Size: 5 inches W x 6¾ inches H
(12.7cm x 17.1cm), excluding ribbon

Skill Level: Advanced

Materials

❑ ½ sheet pastel blue and pastel yellow
7-count plastic canvas
❑ ⅜-inch-wide (9mm) ribbon as listed in color key
❑ 18 x 13mm aquamarine foil-backed oval acrylic
faceted stone
❑ 4 (15 x 7mm) crystal foil-backed navette acrylic
faceted stones
❑ Craft glue or hot-glue gun

Stitching Step by Step

1 Cut one cross each from pastel blue and pastel yellow plastic canvas according to graph (page 32), carefully cutting out gray areas for picot edges and blue areas for weaving ribbon; leave bars indicated by black lines intact.

2 For pastel blue cross, following blue cross ribbon weaving diagram (page 32), thread a 9-inch (22.9cm) length of white ribbon through holes in cross bar, making ends even; trim ends 1¼ inches (3.2cm) from ends of cross, cutting in an inverted V. Thread remaining length from bottom to top, leaving a 1¼ inch-tail cut in an inverted V at bottom. At top, fold ribbon about 1-inch from top of cross and weave remaining length behind vertical ribbon a few bars; trim excess and glue to secure.

3 Using photo as a guide, glue oval and navette stones to front of cross.

4 For pastel yellow cross, following yellow cross ribbon weaving diagram (below), thread a 7½-inch (19cm) length of cream ribbon through holes in cross bar, making ends even; trim ends with a straight edge ½ inch (1.3cm) from ends of cross. Thread remaining length from top to bottom, leaving ½ inch-tails cut in a straight edge.

**Blue Cross Ribbon
Weaving Diagram**

Cross
33 holes x 45 holes
Cut 1 each from pastel blue
and pastel yellow,
cutting out gray
and blue areas

**Yellow Cross Ribbon
Weaving Diagram**

COLOR KEY		
Yards	**³/₈-Inch Ribbon**	
1 (1m)	☐ White	
1 (1m)	☐ Cream	

Laced Bookmarks

Designs by Darla Fanton

Size: **Blue & Yellow:** 1¾ inches W x 8⅞ inches L
(4.4cm x 22.5cm), including yarn tails
Pink & White: 1¾ inches W x 8½ inches L
(4.4cm x 21.6cm), including yarn tails
Red & White: 1¾ inches W x 10 inches L
(4.4cm x 25.4cm), including yarn tails
Skill Level: Beginner

Materials

❏ Small amounts white and yellow
7-count plastic canvas
❏ Uniek Needloft plastic canvas yarn as listed
in color key

Stitching Step by Step

1 Cut plastic canvas according to graphs (page 34).

2 For blue and yellow bookmark and for pink and white bookmark, work vertical rows one at a time, weaving rows of yarn up and down through holes in plastic canvas as shown on graphs, leaving 1-inch (2.5cm) tails extending from both ends of plastic canvas.

3 Follow instructions in step 2 for red and white bookmark, working horizontal rows one at a time.

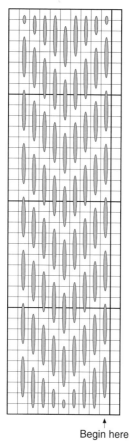

↑
Begin here

Blue & Yellow
11 holes x 38 holes
Cut 1 from yellow

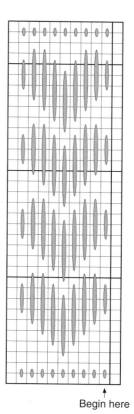

↑
Begin here

Pink & White
11 holes x 34 holes
Cut 1 from white

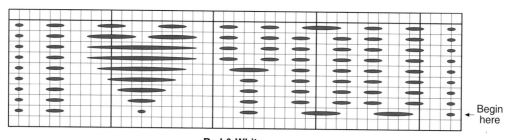

← Begin here

Red & White
44 holes x 11 holes
Cut 1 from white

COLOR KEY

Yards	Plastic Canvas Yarn
4 (3.7m)	■ Christmas red #02
3 (2.8m)	▨ Royal #32
3 (2.8m)	▨ Watermelon #55

Color numbers given are for Uniek
Needloft plastic canvas yarn.

Under the Sea Frame

Design by Jana Britton

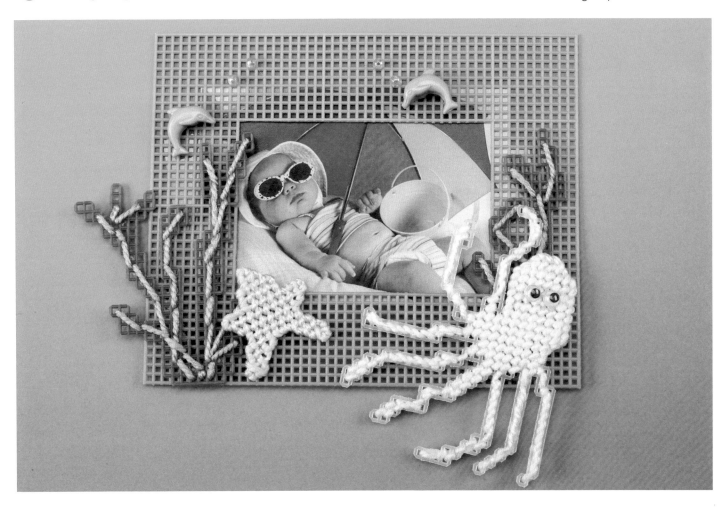

Size: 8⅞ inches W x 7⅝ inches H (22.5cm x 19.4cm), including all embellishments; opening for photo is approximately 4⁷⁄₁₆ inches W x 3 inches H (11.3cm x 7.6cm)

Skill Level: Beginner

Materials

- ❑ ½ sheet turquoise, green and clear 7-count plastic canvas
- ❑ Small amount yellow 7-count plastic canvas
- ❑ Uniek Needloft plastic canvas yarn as listed in color key
- ❑ 2 (7mm) movable eyes
- ❑ 4 crystal opaque and 2 dolphin beads from Sulyn Industries Sparkle Dolphin #54 Beading Fun Pack
- ❑ 5½ x 8¾-inch double-sided PeelnStick adhesive sheet from Therm O Web
- ❑ 7 x 5½-inch (17.8 x 14cm) piece turquoise construction paper
- ❑ Craft glue or hot-glue gun

Stitching Step by Step

1 Cut frame from turquoise plastic canvas, seaweed from green plastic canvas, octopus from clear plastic canvas and starfish from yellow plastic canvas according to graphs (pages 36 and 37). Frame will remain unstitched.

2 Following graphs throughout, stitch and Overcast starfish. Stitch octopus, Overcasting head only.

3 Place large seaweed on left side of frame and small seaweed on right side of frame where indicated with green lines. Stitch in place with a few bottom stitches only, working remaining stitches on seaweed without attaching to frame. Seaweed is not Overcast.

4 Using photo as a guide, tack starfish to frame with yellow. Tack octopus to small seaweed and frame with white, working through all layers.

5 Glue four clear opaque beads and two dolphin beads to frame where indicated.

6 Cut double-sided adhesive sheet to fit construction paper. Following manufacturer's instructions, secure one side of sheet to construction paper and opposite side to photo and back of frame.

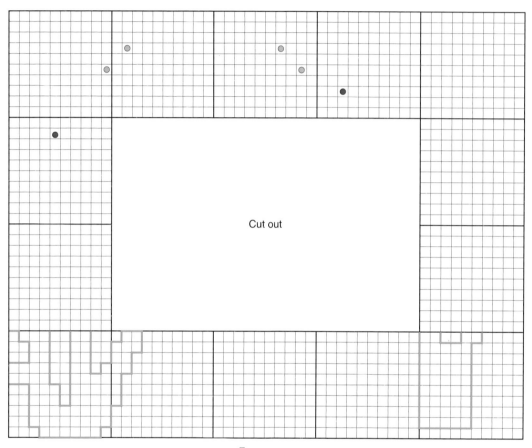

Frame
50 holes x 40 holes
Cut 1 from turquoise
Do not stitch

COLOR KEY	
Yards	**Plastic Canvas Yarn**
4 (3.7m)	☐ White #41
2 (1.9m)	☐ Yellow #57
2 (1.9m)	╱ Fern #23 Backstitch and Straight Stitch
	● Attach movable eye
	○ Attach crystal bead
	● Attach dolphin bead

Color numbers given are for Uniek Needloft plastic canvas yarn.

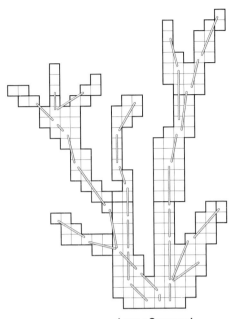

Large Seaweed
21 holes x 28 holes
Cut 1 from green

Octopus
24 holes x 30 holes
Cut 1 from clear

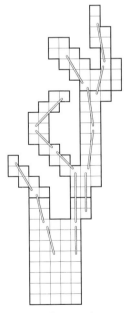

Small Seaweed
11 holes x 28 holes
Cut 1 from green

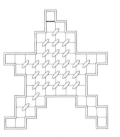

Starfish
10 holes x 11 holes
Cut 1 from yellow

My First Doll House

Designs by Carol Nartowicz

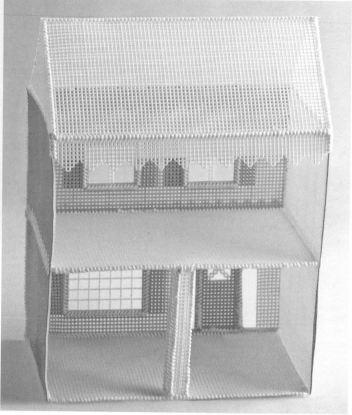

Size:

Doll House: 11⅛ inches W x 14¼ inches H x 7½ inches D (28.3cm x 36.2 x 19cm)

Sofa: 4¼ inches W x 3⅜ inches H x 2 inches D (10.8cm x 8.6cm x 5.1cm)

Living Room Chair: 2¼ inches W x 3⅜ inches H x 2 inches D (5.7cm x 8.6cm x 5.1cm)

Coffee Table: 2¾ inches W x 1½ inches H x 1¾ inches D (7cm x 3.8cm x 4.4cm)

End Table: 1¾ inches square x 1½ inches H (4.4cm x 3.8cm)

Bed: 3⅛ inches W x 4 inches L x 2½ inches H (7.9cm x 10.2cm x 6.4cm)

Dresser: 3¾ inches W x 2⅝ inches H x 2 inches D (9.5cm x 6.7cm x 5.1cm)

Bedroom Chair: 1⅞ inches W x 2¾ inches H x 1⅜ inches D (4.8cm x 7cm x 3.5cm)

Skill Level: Beginner

Materials

❑ 4 sheets each clear 7-count plastic canvas
❑ 3 sheets each lavender and white 7-count plastic canvas
❑ ½ sheet bright pink 7-count plastic canvas
❑ Plastic canvas yarn as listed in color key

Stitching Step by Step

House Cutting

1 Cut one front each from lavender and clear plastic canvas; cut two sides each from lavender and clear plastic canvas according to graphs (pages 40 and 41). Also cut four 70-hole x 49-hole pieces each from clear plastic canvas for floors (no graph).

2 From white plastic canvas, cut one door trim, one large window, two small windows, one front trim, two side trims, two roof ends and two roof trims according to graphs (pages 42 and 43), carefully cutting away gray areas on door trim and large window.

3 Cut two 72-hole x 34-hole pieces for roof front and back and four 4-hole x 34-hole pieces for floor brace pieces from white plastic canvas (no graphs). Cut two 72-hole x 5-hole pieces from clear plastic canvas for roof braces (no graph).

4 Cut one door from bright pink plastic canvas according to graph (page 43), carefully cutting away gray areas. Also from bright pink plastic canvas, cut two 5-hole x 17-holes pieces for large window shutters and four 5-hole x 13-hole pieces for small window shutters (no graphs).

Note: Pieces will remain unstitched except for front and side trim pieces which will be attached to front and side pieces with white Continental Stitches.

House Assembly

1 Use white throughout all assembly and work through all layers of plastic. Following Fig. 1 (page 47) through step 3, place liner behind front. Whipstitch door trim to front around side and top edges where indicated with red lines. Do not stitch bottom edges together at this time. Whipstitch door to door trim where indicated with bright pink lines.

2 Whipstitch top and bottom edges of all windows in place where indicated with green lines. Place shutters next to corresponding windows where indicated with bright pink lines; Whipstitch shutters and side edges of windows in place. Remaining edges of shutters will not be Whipstitched.

3 Place a liner behind each side; Whipstitch front and side pieces together.

4 Following Fig. 2 (page 47) through step 5, place two floor pieces together for each floor. Place corresponding trim on front and side pieces where indicated with blue lines; Whipstitch trim and second floor pieces in place along orange lines with Continental Stitches.

5 Whipstitch first floor pieces to bottom edges of front and side pieces, catching bottom edge of door trim while Whipstitching.

6 Following Fig. 3 (page 47), Whipstitch top edges of roof pieces together; Whipstitch roof ends to roof. Whipstitch top edge of house front to roof and roof trim; Whipstitch roof ends to house sides.

7 Following Fig. 4 (page 47) through step 8, place roof braces behind remaining roof trim, aligning top edges. Whipstitch trim and braces to bottom edge of roof on open side of house. Whipstitch side edges of braces and trim (within brackets) to sides.

8 Whipstitch long edges of floor brace pieces together, forming a column. Center and place brace between top and bottom floors. Whipstitch second floor pieces together and bottom floor pieces together, attaching brace to both floors while Whipstitching.

Furniture Cutting

1 Cut two sofa sides and two living room chair sides from lavender plastic canvas according to graph (page 46).

2 For the living room, cut the following from lavender plastic canvas (no graphs):
One 27-hole x 29 hole piece for sofa front
One 27-hole x 21-hole piece for sofa back
One 27-hole x 12-hole piece for sofa base
One 14-hole x 29-hole piece for chair front
One 14-hole x 21-hole piece for chair back

One 14-hole x 12-hole piece for chair base
One 18-hole x 9-hole piece for coffee table top
One 10-hole x 10-hole piece for end table top

3 For the bedroom, cut the following from lavender plastic canvas (no graphs):
One 20-hole x 26-hole piece for bed top
One 11-hole x 8-hole piece for chair seat
One 24-hole x 12-hole piece for dresser top
Two 22-hole x 4-hole pieces for drawer fronts

4 Cut the following from white plastic canvas according to graphs (pages 44–46):
One each of coffee table front and back
Two coffee table ends
Four end table sides
One headboard
One footboard
Two bed side rails
One bedroom chair front
One bedroom chair back
Two bedroom chair sides
One each of dresser front and back
Two dresser sides

Note: Pieces will remain unstitched.

Furniture Assembly

1 Use white throughout assembly. Following Fig. 5 (page 47) for both sofa and living room chair, Whipstitch sides and back together, then Whipstitch front to sides and back; Whipstitch base to front, back and sides.

2 For coffee table, Whipstitch front and back to ends; Whipstitch front, back and ends to top.

3 For end table, Whipstitch sides together, then Whipstitch sides to top.

4 Following Fig. 6 (page 47) for bed, Whipstitch headboard and footboard to side rails; Whipstitch bed top to top edges of side rails and to headboard and footboard where indicated with blue lines.

5 Following Fig. 7 (page 47) for bedroom chair, Whipstitch front and back to sides; Whipstitch seat to back where indicated with green line and to top edges of front and sides.

6 For dresser, Whipstitch drawer fronts to dresser front where indicated with bright pink lines. Whipstitch front and back to sides; Whipstitch front, back and sides to top.

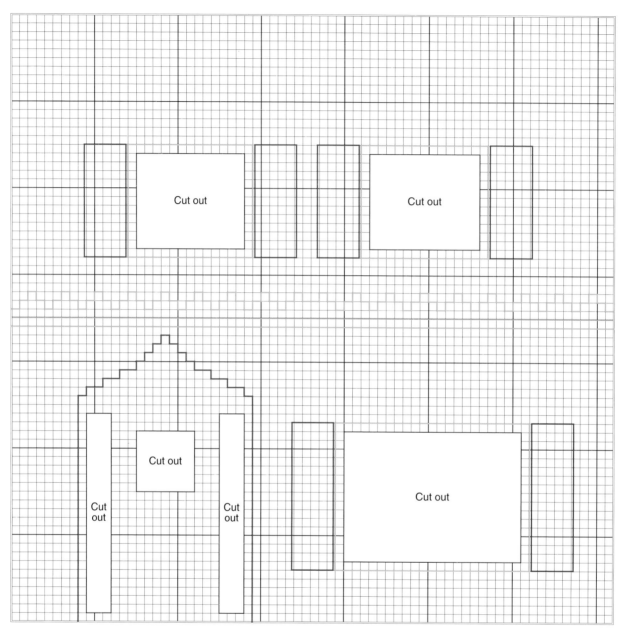

Front
72 holes x 70 holes
Cut 1 from lavender
Cut 1 from clear for liner
Do not stitch

COLOR KEY	
DOLL HOUSE	
Yards	**Plastic Canvas Yarn**
31 (28.4m)	☐ White
	☐ Attach door trim
	☐ Attach window
	☐ Attach door and shutter
	☐ Attach floor
	☐ Attach front and side trim

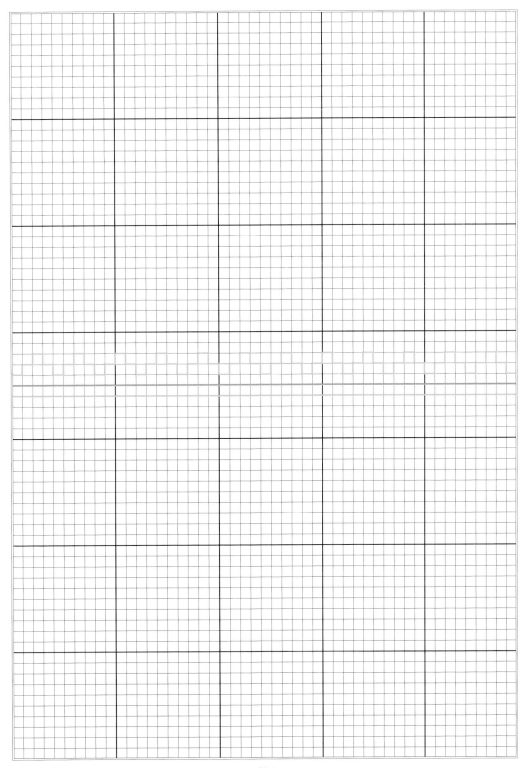

Side
49 holes x 70 holes
Cut 2 from lavender
Cut 2 from clear for liner
Do not stitch

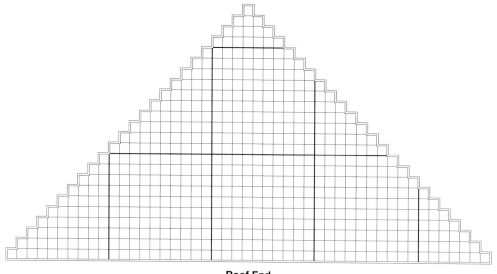

Roof End
47 holes x 24 holes
Cut 2 from white
Do not stitch

Side Trim
49 holes x 4 holes
Cut 2 from white

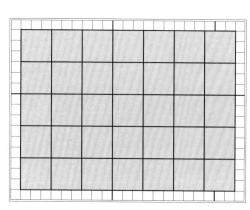

Large Window
23 holes x 17 holes
Cut 1 from white,
carefully cutting
away gray areas
Do not stitch

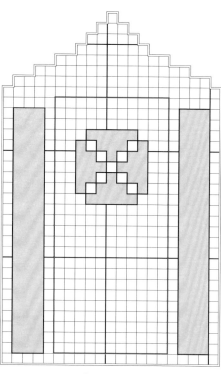

Door Trim
21 holes x 33 holes
Cut 1 from white,
carefully cutting
away gray areas
Do not stitch

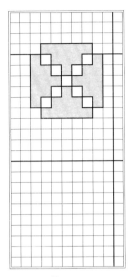

Door
11 holes x 24 holes
Cut 1 from bright pink,
carefully cutting
away gray areas
Do not stitch

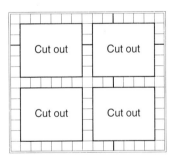

Small Window
15 holes x 13 holes
Cut 2 from white
Do not stitch

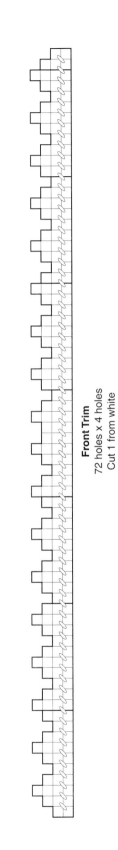

Front Trim
72 holes x 4 holes
Cut 1 from white

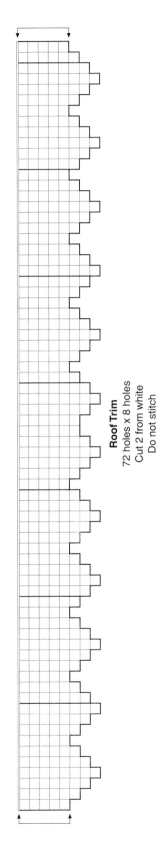

Roof Trim
72 holes x 8 holes
Cut 2 from white
Do not stitch

COLOR KEY
DOLL HOUSE

Yards	Plastic Canvas Yarn
31 (28.4m)	☐ White
	☐ Attach door trim
	☐ Attach window
	☐ Attach door and shutter
	☐ Attach floor
	☐ Attach front and side trim

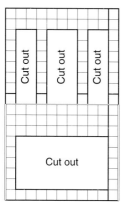

Bedroom Chair Back
11 holes x 18 holes
Cut 1 from white
Do not stitch

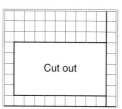

Cut out

Bedroom Chair Front
11 holes x 9 holes
Cut 1 from white
Do not stitch

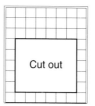

Cut out

Bedroom Chair Side
8 holes x 9 holes
Cut 2 from white
Do not stitch

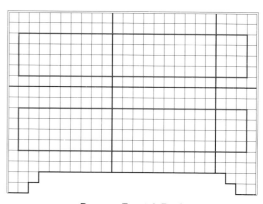

Dresser Front & Back
24 holes x 17 holes
Cut 2 from white
Do not stitch

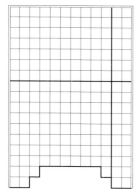

Dresser Side
12 holes x 17 holes
Cut 2 from white
Do not stitch

COLOR KEY	
DOLL HOUSE FURNITURE	
Yards	**Plastic Canvas Yarn**
16 (14.7m)	☐ White
	☐ Attach bed top
	☐ Attach bedroom chair seat
	☐ Attach drawer front

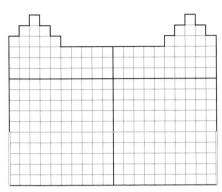

Bed Headboard
20 holes x 16 holes
Cut 1 from white
Do not stitch

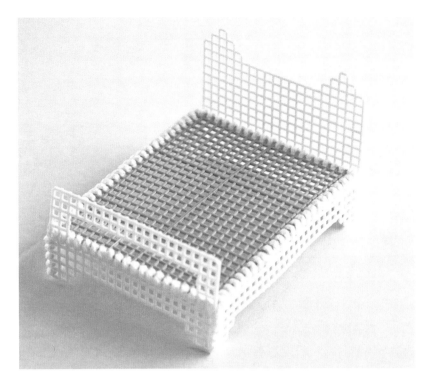

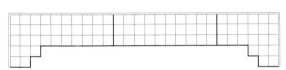

Bed Side Rail
26 holes x 5 holes
Cut 2 from white
Do not stitch

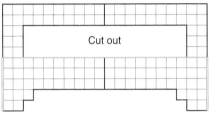

Cut out

Bed Footboard
20 holes x 10 holes
Cut 1 from white
Do not stitch

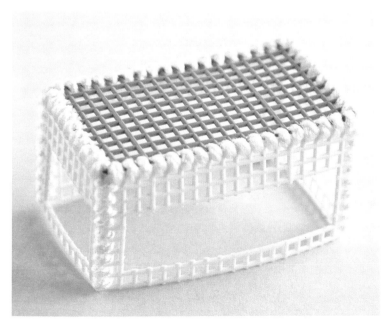

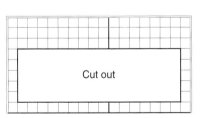

Cut out

Coffee Table Front & Back
18 holes x 9 holes
Cut 2 from white
Do not stitch

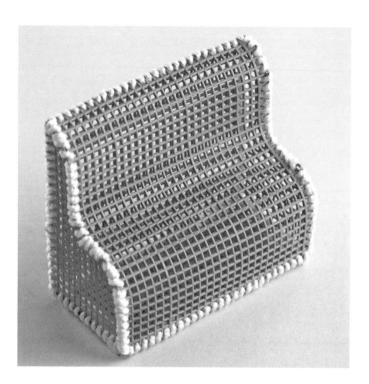

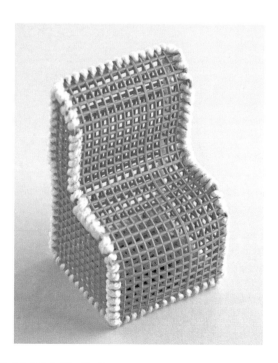

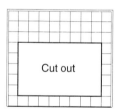

Coffee Table End
10 holes x 9 holes
Cut 2 from white
Do not stitch

End Table Side
10 holes x 9 holes
Cut 4 from white
Do not stitch

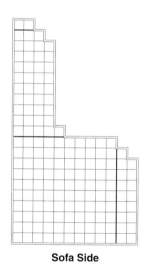

Sofa Side
12 holes x 21 holes
Cut 2 from lavender
Do not stitch

Living Room Chair Side
12 holes x 21 holes
Cut 2 from lavender
Do not stitch

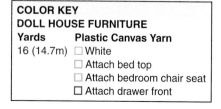

COLOR KEY		
DOLL HOUSE FURNITURE		
Yards	**Plastic Canvas Yarn**	
16 (14.7m)	☐ White	
	☐ Attach bed top	
	☐ Attach bedroom chair seat	
	☐ Attach drawer front	

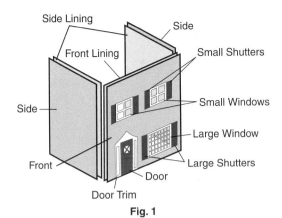

Fig. 1

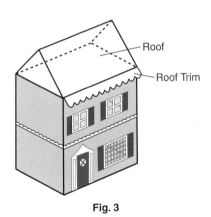

Fig. 2

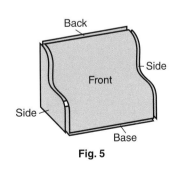

Fig. 3

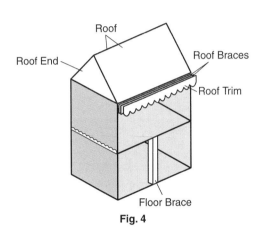

Fig. 4

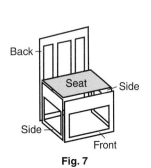

Fig. 5

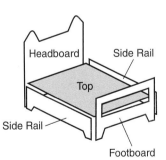

Fig. 6

Fig. 7

Annie's Attic®

**CUSTOMER SERVICE AND
TOLL-FREE ORDER LINE**
or to request a free catalog
(800) 582-6643
Visit AnniesAttic.com

We have made every effort to ensure
the accuracy and completeness of these
instructions. We cannot, however, be
responsible for human error, typographical
mistakes or variations in individual work.

ISBN: 978-1-57367-350-1
Printed in USA

1 2 3 4 5 6 7 8 9

Shopping for Supplies

For supplies, first shop your local craft
and needlework stores. Some supplies
may be found in fabric, hardware and
discount stores. If you are unable to find
the supplies you need, please call Annie's
Attic at (800) 582-6643 to request a free
catalog that sells plastic canvas supplies.

Getting Started

Before You Cut

Buy one brand of canvas for each entire project as brands can differ slightly in the distance between bars. Count holes carefully from the graph before you cut, using the bolder lines that show each 10 holes. These 10-count lines begin from the left side for vertical lines and from the bottom for horizontal lines. Mark canvas before cutting; then remove all marks completely before stitching. If the piece is cut in a rectangular or square shape and is either not worked, or worked with only one color and one type of stitch, the graph is not included in the pattern. Instead, the cutting and stitching instructions are given in the general instructions or with the individual project instructions.

Covering the Canvas

Bring needle up from back of work, leaving a short length of yarn on back of canvas; work over short length to secure. To end a thread, weave needle and thread through the wrong side of your last few stitches; clip. Follow the numbers on the small graphs beside each stitch illustration; bring your needle up from the back of the work on odd numbers and down through the front of the work on even numbers. Work embroidery stitches last, after the canvas has been completely covered by the needlepoint stitches.

Basic Stitches

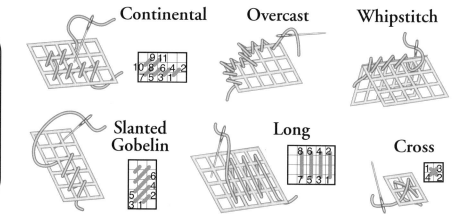

Continental Overcast Whipstitch

Slanted Gobelin Long Cross

Embroidery Stitches

French Knot  Lazy Daisy Backstitch Straight

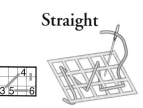

METRIC KEY:
millimeters = (mm)
centimeters = (cm)
meters = (m)
grams = (g)